MORE DIMOND GEMS

Memories of a Dorset Farmer

BY

JACK DIMOND

ACKNOWLEDGEMENTS

I would, once again, like to express my grateful thanks to the following people, who have given of their time and knowledge, and provided articles and photographs for me to use. They are; Diane Simpson, Sherborne Museum, Nancy Cook, Jack and Jean Treasure, Ann Rossiter, Valerie Mitchell, Richard Hole, Girly Hole, Larry Skeats, Ken Fox, John Stranger, Richard Wood, Pat Jenkins, Tom Curry, Ted Warry, Mrs.H.Hansell, Mrs.G.Rogers, The Farmers' Women's Club, John Smith, Brian Lock, The Young Farmers Club County organiser, the Castleton Waterwheel Restoration Society, Mrs. Ann Smith - the Castle Estates Archivist, Kathryn Barker, Graham Lock, Tony Young, Basil Cane, and to Jenny Cane for all the typing and production of a working draught again.

And lastly, my gratitude, once again, to my wife Diana, for her tolerance and encouragement, and to all my family, especially Robert and Christina Dimond, Ian and Dawn Dimond, Richard Dimond, and Georgina Dimond for their patience and permission to use their stories.

INTRODUCTION

I have found my second book a bit more difficult to piece together.

It is based on all those stories, both happy and sad, that I remember. The long hours we worked used to be rewarded by meeting up with our farming friends. Most of us usually had a story or two to tell. This was what made it all worthwhile.

Today, with all those farmers having to sell up, and the traditional markets disappearing, the few that will be left will find themselves much more isolated, especially when they live miles from anyone, down a country lane. I cannot see the next generation enjoying farming and the country life the way I used to.

If you do not have a sense of humour, read no further.

Jack Dimond
Sherborne. 2003

FOREWORD

To call Jack Dimond a character is an insult, the term has been devalued. Jack Dimond, who I have known for many years, is Jack Dimond; a well respected and loved, true son of Dorset farming. It is a great pity that Jack's innate good taste and decency have prevented him from telling his more racy anecdotes, with which he has entertained us over the years, but that aside, this is how farming used to be before we became hide-bound by form filling and bureaucracy. In some ways it is a great pity that each generation has to start from scratch, learning from its own mistakes and triumphs. In the future somebody might develop a superplug to transfer the wisdom and experience of the older generation to the young, but would they use it properly? I doubt it. Until such time, we have the next best thing, books such as this one.

Many people say they are going to write a book when they retire; few of us have the drive to actually start, let alone follow one successful volume with another. Well, Jack has and he puts us all to shame. In centuries to come when a Dimond asks "What was a farm? What did a farmer do?" he will be handed Jack's dusty tome and told "read this". History books tend to dwell on the lives of kings and princes. This book is written by a true prince of Dorset farming, a man admired for his ability to farm and for his love of the countryside, long before the term "environmentally friendly farming" was coined. Read and enjoy: I am sure you will.

Richard Wood
Group Secretary Sherborne NFU

LIST OF PHOTOGRAPHS

CONTENTS

Sherborne Castles – taken from the railway bridge
looking across our farm

CHAPTER 1

Living in the Country

I was born on a small farm, in a little hamlet called Pilsdon, near Bridport. I think I have been very lucky to have lived all my life on a farm in this lovely county of Dorset. I have spent the last 72 years living at Castle Farm, Sherborne, which overlooks two castles, (*see photo*), the old one, which is 12th Century, (*on the right of the photo*), and the new one, built in 1594, (*on the left of the photo*). We also have Sherborne Abbey, (see photo) in the centre of our town. A church has stood on this site for over one thousand years. All three are under ten minutes walk from our house. If you ever come to Sherborne, you should pay all three a visit.

Most families that lived in the country, and a few in towns, had their own hens for eggs, and chickens for

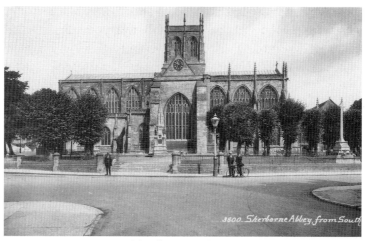

Sherborne Abbey

Sunday dinners. A lot kept a pig as well, probably given to them by a farmer. If he had a sow with more young than it could cope, he would give the piglets away to save their lives.

All those different animals we used to keep on our farms. You only had to walk into a farmyard, and the first thing you saw were hens and cockerels, ducks and geese, sows with their young, four or five cart horses in the stable, the farmer and his wife and children hand milking cows in the barn, a goat or two running around, a few calves suckling their mothers, and all those milk churns on the milk stands. That was in the days when the farmers and their families worked long hours. A farmer works a 70 hour week providing food for other people's table as well as his own. I don't think there can be any other occupation that has its ups and downs like farming. That's why a lot of farmers will tell you they are not making any money. If you put a sign up 'Eggs for Sale' you are on call 24 hours a day, and if you rent a farm, when the time comes to sell up you and your family will have nowhere to live as it is a tied house. Also, apart from the government pension, the farmer has no company pension to live on.

I started our pedigree herd of Holsteins in 1958, for the very good reason that they produced more milk than our old herd of short horns. At that time I had 75 cows and one bull. Over the years this has increased to 145 milking cows, with followers, and several bulls (*see photo*).

In my day almost every farm worker kept a pig or two and some laying hens, all fed on scraps from the kitchen. Now I doubt if you will find six farmers in Dorset who own a pig. We all knew the way to kill a pig on the premises, and prepare the food. This was when we knew what we were eating, and where it came from. Everything on a pig is edible, right down to its tail. I have spent hours cleaning out the stomach guts of a pig, and turning them inside-out with a smooth stick, putting them in a bucket of salt water overnight, plaiting them up the next morning and my mother fried them for breakfast. What a good start to the day. They were called chidlings. Today you have to pay someone to dispose of them. What a waste, and what about all those empty farm buildings around the countryside today!

I heard only the other day, a poultry farmer with several thousand laying hens for sale, just one year old,

Dorset   Midnight   Helena
↙   ↓   ↘
Herd prefix   Sire (Father)   Family Name

Dorset Midnight Helena was born on the 3rd June 1990. She has given us some lovely heifer (female) calves, like the one on the front cover. She is one of the best cows we have had at Castle Farm. She is classified as EX93 by the British Holstein (Friesian) Society. We know her as Number 10. In her lifetime so far she has given over 100 tons of milk (over 175,000 pints). She had her 10th calf (a heifer) on July 25th 2003.

4

eventually had to pay someone 50p a bird to take them off his hands to be dumped. What a crazy world we live in. I dread to think what my mother and father would have said, as we must have eaten hundreds of old boiler hens when we were younger.

A boiler hen is a hen that has come to the end of her laying life. All the feathers were used to go in our beds as feather mattresses, which were far more comfortable than those we lay on today.

Not many farmers have a hobby. In the winter months they might have a few days shooting with their friends. Before they go out, they have to milk the cows and feed the rest of the cattle – probably five hours' work. At the end of the day's shooting they come home and do it all over again. There are still people who believe milk comes in plastic bottles from supermarkets!

Have you noticed all those roadside hedges? They are gradually meeting from one side to the other like a tunnel. This has only come about because the councils and the farmers can no longer afford the time or the money to cut them. Gone are the days of the 'cut and laid' hedges. This practice is now a dying art, and few farmers do it as it is very labour intensive. In less than five years we will need the head lights on our cars day and night on all country roads, and even if you could see over the hedges, you will not see many animals. In 5 years time most of the green fields will be full of docks, thistles and stinging nettles.

We were shooting one day, when one of our guns shot a cock pheasant, which dropped in a patch of brambles. He and one of our lady beaters went to look for it. After a good ten minutes this lady beater shouted out, "It's OK, I've got your cock in my hand." I think it must have played on the gentleman's mind, because he never hit another bird the rest of the day.

I was talking to a friend of mine the other day, and he told me he was off to give a talk to a Nudist Camp. On his way down the lane to the camp he came across a man who was wearing nothing but a pair of Wellington boots. He was in the bushes wrestling with a ewe. He pulled his car over and asked him if he needed a hand. "No, no," he shouted, "I can manage." My friend asked "Are you shearing?" "No, no, no," he shouted back. "I don' wanna sharin', you go on an' catch yer own."

CHAPTER 2

My Lucky Escape

For us, time-sharing meant togetherness, not holidays. We only had one holiday a year by the sea, which we had to save up for. I remember if I had 1/6d, (7p), I was very well off.

On one Sunday school outing to Weymouth I nearly lost my life. Four girls in our party hired a small rowing boat for one hour. After about twenty minutes they were fed up, so they said we could finish out the hour. Four of us said yes, we would – Norman Cheney, Leslie Barter, Dennis Barter (Trucker) and I. We had not gone far when one of us lost an oar. It became so difficult to carry on with just the one. As we drifted further out to sea we all panicked. Leslie Barter and Dennis jumped out. That was the last we saw of them until 7 o'clock that night, as they were spotted by fishermen about three miles out to sea, Trucker ended up in the Red Cross hut on the sands, where they had to pump his stomach out. We learned later he had about three gallons of water in his stomach, and we were told he was very lucky to have survived.

This left only Norman (Podgy) Cheney and me in the boat. Podgy, as we all called him, was in such a state he must have shouted, "Mother", over one hundred times. By this time the waves looked about ten feet high. We were bobbing about like a cork. I was in such a state I jumped over the side, although I could not swim. I shall never know why I did it. It must have been a million to one chance I came up the other side of the boat, and Podgy dragged me back in.

For the next three hours we drifted further out to sea. We could not see land, but the sea became a bit calmer, and we managed to get some of the water out of the boat. All of a sudden we spotted the chalk hill carving of the white horse at Osmington on the coast in Weymouth bay. The tide must have changed and we got washed up on the pebble beach near there. We were not long jumping out of that damned boat. We ran like hell hoping to find where we started from. After fifteen minutes of running, we came across some of our party. As we were both wet through, one of the girls went up into the town and bought us a pair of new trunks each to go home in. We asked if they had seen 'Trucker' Barter. They said, "No". So we panicked again. Our teacher in charge of us went over to the Red Cross hut, and poor Trucker was in there, sat in a chair, white as a ghost. We were all pleased to see one another again.

Our coach left Weymouth at 8 o'clock for Sherborne, and we all went home together. All four of us said we never wanted to see Weymouth again. When we got off that coach our parents were there to collect us, as they had read the news in the Sherborne evening paper 'FOUR BOYS NEARLY DROWNED AT WEYMOUTH - LESLIE BARTER, DENNIS BARTER, NORMAN CHENEY AND JACK DIMOND.' They were all so pleased to see us get off that coach. I remember I had my biggest telling off ever, as when we had left that morning, the last words my mother had said to me, "Now don't you go getting on any boat." That was a day I shall never forget.

As a lad I can remember walking miles to find a Horse Chestnut tree. We used to spend hours playing 'conkers'. We would drill a hole through a conker, then tie a knot on a piece of cord and thread it through the hole. We would then hold it up by the cord hoping our opponent could not smash it off with theirs (*see photo*). Today not many young lads would know what a Horse Chestnut was. We had to make our own entertainment back then.

A lot of us used to play marbles. They came in all colours, and sometimes we would swap a colour with a mate for one we didn't have. We also used to play hopscotch at school playtime and a lot of us kids used to play hoop-la too, and the girls often used to use a skipping rope and skip to school. On Saturdays in the winter we would be playing 'Fox and Hounds', giving someone a good ten minutes head start then the rest of us would give chase. We ran for miles. It kept us very fit. Today, most of the youngsters spend their time on

Playing 'conkers'

computers or mobile phones. Not a very healthy activity.

I was out walking in the fields one summer's night, and met up with a farmer's daughter who lived in the next village from us. It was a very hot night and it started to thunder, so we both headed off for the closest hay rick for shelter. She had beautiful blonde hair and we were both sixteen. We must have worn ourselves out snogging, as we both dropped off to sleep. I think it must have been a new experience for both of us. When we woke up the moon was shining and it was rather late. She said she must run off home as quickly as she could as her father might have the Police out looking for her. When I was on my way home, I spotted two policemen out in the road. It was then I saw her father come around the corner on his bicycle. He had called Sherborne Police Station and told them his daughter was missing.

Half the village was out looking for her too. I remember I hid in the hedge for a good hour, and then made my way home. Her father was on our doorstep the next morning looking for me. I promised we would not be out so late next time, and he let me off. Aah, the innocence of youth!

We were on holiday a few years ago, when, one evening after dinner, about eight of us were sat round a table in the hotel lounge, when a lady in our party suggested we could all play a game which she called 'Funny Experiences'. So we took it in turns. When it came to this young lady's turn to tell us her story she told us she had been engaged to be married three times, but had never been lucky. She said she worked in town, and walked to work every morning. She always walked past a tall dark, handsome young man who said 'good morning' to her every day. He was walking in the opposite direction. She thought to herself 'don't I ever fancy you!' Then one day, out of the blue, he rang her up at work, asking her if she was the young lady he said good morning to every day. She nearly fell down the phone. When she had recovered her composure she said she was. He asked her if she was free one evening as he would like to take her out. She said, "Yes, I would like to very much." So off she went and bought herself a very nice dark, almost see-through dress. A week later he agreed to pick her up on the Saturday night at 8 o'clock. With Christmas only a week away she was hoping for her best Christmas ever. He took her to a very nice restaurant out in the country. They sat at a table for two in a dark corner. It was then he gave her a lovely rose. She became so excited she leaned over and gave him a kiss on the cheek. As she moved away she had his wig swinging from one of her earrings. She was so embarrassed she could have died. He never had one hair on his head, and was a man in his fifties. We all had a good laugh.

I only heard the other day of a young girl asking her boyfriend to come and stay for the weekend, as her Mum and Dad were going away for two nights. He thought he had better go prepared so he went into the chemist shop and asked the man at the counter if he could have four packets. At the weekend he arrived at the girlfriend's house. She answered the door and told him it was not very good news, as her Mum and Dad had decided not to go away. She said, "Do come in and meet them." So in he goes, feeling very shy. After having a cup of coffee she said, "Let's go for a walk." So off they go. After a few minutes she noticed he did not look very well. She said, "Is there anything wrong?" "Yes" he said, "you did not tell me your father worked in a chemist shop."

CHAPTER 3

Early Days

We all survived. I was born before penicillin, television, polio jabs, frozen foods, contact lenses and the pill! I was born before radar, credit cards, split atoms, and laser beams. Before tights, spin-dryers, electric blankets, dish-washers, and air-conditioning. Computers or hardware did not exist. Hardware meant hard wear, and software wasn't even a word. In 1944 'made in Japan' meant shoddy workmanship, and the term 'making out' referred to how you did in an exam. Pizzas, MacDonald's, Chinese take-away and instant coffee were still to come. The only toilet paper we had was an old newspaper, after it had been used for a table-cloth. Smack was what we had across the ass. Today it is a drug taken for pleasure. I was born before men walked on the moon. We got married first, and then lived together afterwards. In our time, having a meaningful relationship meant getting on with our cousins, while designer jeans were for scheming girls. We thought 'fast food' was what we ate in Lent, and 'outer space' was a back seat at the cinema. I was born before gay rights, computer dating, and mortgages. If we saw men wearing ear-rings, we thought they were changing sex, and if we saw young girls wearing jeans we thought they must be land girls. We always thought a 'green belt' was something we wore. Now we are told it is a strip of land surrounding a town!

Can you remember all those socks our mothers used to knit with four needles, and having to sit for ages with our arms out while she wound the wool into a ball from the hank she'd bought at the local market? It looked very complicated. I remember the socks she knitted, and all the ones she had to darn on something that looked like a wooden mushroom. What about all the shirt collars that were turned when they started to fray, and when the sheets were worn, they were initially turned side to centre for a bit longer, then made into handkerchiefs and table napkins. Pullovers and cardigans were all knitted by hand. The women made good use of what little spare time they had in those days, and home/hand made clothes usually lasted longer, and saved money.

If a young man got a girl in trouble, he was probably put in a mental home. In 1942 the Royal Naval Auxiliary Hospital was established in Coldharbour, Sherborne. It was the Royal Navy's only orthopaedic hospital in the country. After the war it was used as a mental home, and being only half a mile from our farm, I used to collect six or seven of the lads for a day's threshing. I said to one of them, one day, "How ever did you happen to end up in a place like this?" He said, "I accidentally got a girl in trouble. She ended up having twins, so I was sent to this place. I think I should have had a medal, because I've only got one nacker!"

Knickers were called 'bloomers' or, more rudely, 'passion-killers' in the fifties, the birth-rate rose by 10%, then someone introduced tights, and the rate went back down again. Condoms were just coming on the market. I remember I was up at Sherborne's Pack Monday Fair with a friend of mine, who was two or three years older than me. A man on one of the stalls asked us if we would like to buy some. I hardly knew what they were, but my mate said he would try some. I remember they were 50 for 1/- (5p)! They must have been OK because he never had to get married.

A few years ago the landlord of a local public house told me one of the best investments he had ever made was to install two dispensing machines in the Gents toilets. He told me he made more money from the machine nearest the door for the simple reason he never stocked it up! When the young lads put their £1 coins in and couldn't get anything out, they were too embarrassed to ask for their money back. The contents of that machine was all clear profit.

We had never heard of a banana split as we only had oranges, nuts and bananas at Christmas. We thought having a shower was a storm of rain, and a dish-washer was a good pair of hands. Washing-up detergents were yet to come. Paper cups and plates, and plastic knives and forks were never heard of. Plastic bags and pipes were never seen.

Motorways were yet to come, and a roundabout was something we had a ride on at the fair. The only 'cats' eyes' we ever saw was at night when a cat ran across the road. We thought a zebra crossing was something we saw in a zoo, not on a busy road, and a sleeping policeman was a tired bobby, not a lump of tarmac to slow you down. Whoever thought we would have to pay to park our car in our town.

I wonder how many people there are in the town who know where their water comes from when they turn on the tap. Before 1852, Sherborne, like many other towns in England suffered periodic outbreaks of cholera and typhoid through the lack of a clean water supply. It comes from three bore holes not a stone's throw from our back door. In 1852 a Robert John Dymond, (a coincidence), an engineering surveyor from Exeter, drew up plans for Sherborne's local Health Board to pump water from a borehole at Castleton, on the edge of the town, to a reservoir north of the town. Unfortunately his system failed, so John Lawson, a local civil engineer was employed. He designed a 26 foot diameter waterwheel with buckets fed by two boreholes, 35 feet and 45 feet deep, housed in a Pump House (*see photo*) to feed the reservoir, located on the corner of Bristol Road and St. Aldhelm's Road, by the Gryphon School. Water was taken from Sherborne Lake and the Coombe stream from which Sherborne gets its name – 'cire burne' meaning 'clear stream'.

The Original Sherborne Pumping Station House

In 1848 Sherborne had 14 breweries, 11 slaughterhouses and 11 laundries for the big houses and estates. The population in Sherborne in 1861 was 5,793, in 1,119 dwelling houses. Although the work was started in 1856, it was not completed until 1869, when water was available to residents from 6.30 am to 8.00 am and 5.30 pm to 7.00 pm, a total of three hours per day. Houses were charged 1d per tap, large houses having one tap, smaller houses and cottages sharing a tap between four or six of them. The charge was increased to 2d in 1874. In 1876 a third borehole of 50 feet was sunk, although only two are in use at any one time, and their overall depth has been increased to 360 feet. A new pump house was built at that time, replacing the old one, for the new steam driven wheel. Responsibility for Sherborne's water supply had been with the local Board of Health until 1895 when Sherborne Urban District Council was formed, and they managed it until its closure in 1959. Between 1912 and 1926 water was available from 7.00 am to 9.00 pm – a total of 14 hours a day. In May 1959, six months short of 90 years, the Pumping Station was closed for good, water distribution being done by the newly installed electric immersible pumps, which can pump 35,000 gallons of water per hour. Sherborne's water is hard but pure and has no chlorine in it. In 1963 Wessex Water Board took over the responsibility of supplying Sherborne with water.

As part of Sherborne's Industrial Heritage the Castleton Water Wheel Restoration Society was formed in 1975 and the site first opened to the public in 1985. It

The 1940 Pump House to supply Haydon Camp -
note our farmhouse in the background

now has regular Open Days from May to October, when you can see the ongoing work.

In the late thirties, I helped to lay a six inch cast iron pipe from a smaller pump house (*see photo*) next to Sherborne Pumping Station House in Castleton to Haydon Camp, to supply it with mains water. They were eighteen feet in length and weighed about 6cwt each. It was nearly two hundred tons to go all that way. We put them in a three foot trench, most of which was dug by hand. It was about two miles long and took about four months to dig. I remember turning on the tap to check every joint for leaks. The camp (*see photos*) was originally built for the American Army Hospital, and in the six days following D Day, 6th June 1944, the hospital treated over 3,000 wounded allied soldiers. After the US Army left it became a holding camp for Polish refugees.

The Army Chapel, Haydon Camp

On Parade at Haydon Camp

After the war a lot of those Poles worked on farms, got married, and did not return home. We had one apply for a job one day. He said he lived in Chard, so he came up for an interview. He arrived three hours late. He said he could not find Sherborne! He ended up a few miles west of Salisbury, and he found Sherborne on his way home. He arrived on an old motor-bike and side-car with his wife and two kids. He ended up getting the job. They were some of the best workers you could get.

We had another farm worker apply for a job, so up he came for an interview. He was a short, stockily built chap, and my father gave him the job. The farmer usually supplied a cattle lorry to move their furniture. The day he and his wife arrived, (or so we thought), the first thing that came down the tail-board was five kids, so up goes Father, as the man had told him at the interview it was only he and his wife. After taking a closer look at this man, my father realised it was not the same man he had agreed to hire for the job. After having a chat about his interview, the man admitted he had not come up himself, but had sent his brother instead. I remember Father saying he could not drive those five kids up that tail-board and send them back, so he kept the man.

On September 30th 1940 over 300 bombs were dropped on Sherborne just before 4 o'clock in the afternoon. By some miracle only eighteen people lost their lives, and none of the historic buildings within the town were seriously damaged, although many houses and water and sewage services were ruined. The very first bomb that fell killed one of our farming friends, Horace Legg. He farmed Silver Lake Farm at Bradford

Abbas. He was cutting thistles with a scythe with one of his men down by the railway line, which ran through his property. The workman just threw himself to the ground, and luckily escaped any harm, but Horace ran for the ditch and was hit by shrapnel. My old infant school in Newland had a direct hit (*see photo*). Luckily the forty youngsters and my old school mistress, Miss Percy, had just left for home two minutes before the bombs dropped.

Our coalman, Charlie Bow, was delivering coal with his horse and cart at the bottom of North Road. He heard the bombs falling, so he laid on the pavement under someone's window when it fell out on him, so he jumped into the front room for cover. When it was all over he found his horse had been hit by shrapnel and had to be put down.

We were hand milking our cows when the air raid siren sounded. It was mounted on scaffolding behind the Police Station in Digby Road. We all ran to our air raid shelter in the garden. For ten minutes everything shook. I shall never forget it. When the 'all clear' sounded out we came again. To our surprise our house was still standing. The closest bomb we had was about 100 yards away in Oborne Road, where a Mr. Jimmy Lintern's bungalow took a direct hit.

We walked into town that night to see the damage. We had a job to recognise any of our streets. The whole town was without water and electricity for days. We had to fetch our water from a spring which was on our farm. Our two neighbours, Mr. & Mrs. Hann, had a daughter living in Lenthay. Her name was Mrs. Gray. We knew her well. Several bombs fell in that area, and her house

My sister Nancy & friends outside Newland Infant School

was badly damaged, so they had to move out. As they had nowhere to go, and we had an empty farm cottage at the time, my father offered it to them. He told them he would fetch their furniture the next day with his horse and wagon. As we arrived we saw two men digging in a trench outside their front door. There was barely enough room to reverse the wagon back. We had only just started to load up when one of the men shouted he had found a bomb, and there it was, only a few feet from the horse. They told us it was still ticking. We were not long moving away from there. All we'd had time to collect were two beds. The area was soon evacuated and the bomb defused. We went back at a later date for the rest of the furniture. Those of us still remaining in town will always remember that day, and how lucky we were.

We always say 'something good often comes out of something bad'. Towards the end of the war we were very short of food. There was a slaughter man in Sherborne who made a good living selling meat on the black market. We all knew him very well, as he often did odd jobs for us.

One Sunday afternoon he set off on the Southern National bus from Greenhill, Sherborne to kill a cow. He told us he was sat at the back of the bus when he spotted a police car which seemed to be following him. So he got off the bus in Milborne Port and got on another bus coming back to Sherborne. He said he had not been sat down in his house more than ten minutes when there was a knock at the door. It was the police. They asked him if he was on a Sunday afternoon joy ride? He just told them he had forgotten something. That was just one of the many close shaves he had.

Another time he and a mate of his had killed a cow on a farm just outside town. A few days later they went back to joint it up. When they had finished they thought the safest place to put it was in the ten milk churns which were in the dairy. They had just put the lid on the last churn when they spotted a police car coming down the farm track. They both shot up the ladder into the loft above, managed to pull the ladder up, and let the trap door back down. He told us they both stayed up there for two days and nights. If the police had lifted one of those churn covers they would both have been caught.

An elderly lady told me one day she had spent over 40 years working as a midwife in several large hospitals. I asked her if she was in favour of the husbands attending the birth, she said "definitely not, I was delivering a baby one day, the husband was sat in a chair watching, he was as white as a ghost and never said a word. When this baby popped out it was jet black. He flew out of that chair in a raging temper. Dragging his wife out of bed by the hair".

CHAPTER 4

Making our own fun

One of our greatest pleasures, living on a farm, was catching wild rabbits. It was great fun, especially at harvest time, when we were cutting corn by a machine we called a binder. In those days, as we were getting closer to the middle of the field, the rabbits would start to come out. With all those bundles of corn lying on the ground, they were so confused, and could not run quite so fast.

I remember we were cutting a field of wheat up by Castletown Way, in Sherborne, and about 4 o'clock that afternoon fifty or sixty boys and girls came over from the Council School to have some fun. They all brought a stick. A man had been watching us for several hours down by the gate. When the rabbits started to run out, this man walked over with a gun under his arm and asked my father if he was the farmer. He said he was. The man asked him if he had seen any partridges. My father said, "Could be one or two in there." After telling Father he was the head keeper on the estate he told him to order all those kids out of the field. My father immediately said, "The only one I am going to send off is you, as I was here before you came, and I will probably still be here after you've gone." The man slowly walked out, and my father enjoyed watching all those kids having great fun. After the field was all cut, the rabbits would be shared out. As the older and faster runners would probably knock down ten or fifteen rabbits each, and the younger ones not do so well, Father would see as many kids as possible went home with a rabbit. I remember some days they could kill as many as a hundred.

Almost all young lads that lived in the country started off having an air-gun for Christmas then went on to a .410 and after that it was a 12 bore shot-gun. By then you were a first class shot. One night I remember my father shot 23 rabbits with 24 cartridges and he always said he would have found the other one if it hadn't got dark quite so quickly. Most all country folk lived on wild rabbits, especially through the war years. I remember the very spot where I caught my first rabbit in a wire, and I must have caught hundreds after that. They would sell at 4d to 6d (2-2$^1/_2$ p) each. I used to take mine up to Mould & Edwards in Cheap Street, in Sherborne, almost every week, as this was part of my wages. Working on the farm, if you sold rabbits off the farm today, the tax man would be after you.

In those days you could catch rabbits in a gin (trap), (*see photo*). I had over fifty. I moved them around in the burrows all through the winter months. I was off out one Sunday morning to move them onto fresh burrows, when my sister Nancy thought she would come and give me a hand. She thought it would be a good idea to carry one from hole to hole without releasing the spring. She started to walk with this gin in her hand, when it accidentally swung against her leg. As she fell down in the stinging nettles the gin went off, and it was clamped on the lower part of her ass. It was the largest thing I have ever caught in a gin! It was a very painful experience for her and it took ten minutes to get it off. Nancy never came out to catch rabbits in gins with me again. Today it would be illegal to set one.

Catching rabbits with ferrets was also great fun. Almost every country lad went out ferreting. We would put the net over the hole of the burrows, and then put the ferret in. After a minute or two you could hear a rumble under the ground, then out the rabbits would come into the nets, (*see photo*) with the ferret tight behind them. You jumped in as quickly as you could to catch the rabbit and take it out of the net then set the net again, hoping another would be coming out. If the ferret failed to come out, you knew it had killed one underground. We always kept a large dog ferret that we would put on a line and send in. After hopefully finding it we would dig them out. Sometimes you might not ever find it that day, so we would stop in all the holes in the burrow bar one, and fasten a bag of straw in the mouth of that hole with a rabbit's liver in the bag hoping you would lure it out. I

A Gin Trap

Out Ferreting

remember going out on dark winters nights to check that bag. You usually found it.

We lost one once for six weeks, then one afternoon we saw six or seven rooks soaring over something out in the field. My father said, "I bet they've spotted that ferret", so out he went. Sure enough, that same ferret was out there in the grass. It was one of the quietest ones we had 'til that day. The minute it was caught it ran up my father's arm and grabbed on the lower half of his ear. Before he could release it, it drew blood. He eventually got it off. He was in so much pain; I remember him saying he got a good stick from the hedge and killed the bugger.

As a young lad, our son Richard had a lot of fun as a member of the local Pony Club. Each year, in October, the Prince Philip Cup Mounted Games were held during the Horse of the Year Show at the Empire Pool, Wembley, London. The competitors have to be members of their local Pony Club, under the age of 16 years, and their ponies have to measure 14.2 h.h. and under (that's 14.2 hands, a hand being 4 inches). They are picked by someone at their local club who is prepared to spend many hours training them.

In February 1965 Mrs. Harding selected a team of five boys and girls from the Blackmore Vale Club. They were Barry Mogg, Linda Hoit, Elsie Courage, Sue Chaffey and Richard Dimond. To qualify for Wembley they had to win the two preliminary rounds. So, dreaming of Wembley, we started to practice each week. There are fifteen different games in the final which the team had to master.

They are:-

1) The Mug Race.
2) The Rope Race.
3) The Egg and Spoon Race.
4) The Potato Picking Scramble.
5) Stepping Stone Dash.
6) Litter Race.
7) The Sack Race.
8) Uncle Tom Cobley Stakes.
9) Flag Race.
10) Team Relay Bending Race.
11) Musical Sacks (Pairs).
12) Motor Tyre Race.
13) The Postmen's Chase.
14) The Anti-Litter Campaign.
15) The Sharpshooters' Race.

By July those five youngsters were winning almost every class at all the local gymkhanas, so we thought they were in with a good chance of winning their Preliminary round, which was held at Farley Castle. They were up against eighteen teams of five, four members of each team competing in every event. Six clubs were in each heat, and points were awarded for their placings. Blackmore Vale came out the winners at Farley Castle which meant they qualified to go on to the Zone final at Butlin's Holiday Camp, Minehead, in August where they met five other teams. They were doing well, and by the end of the day, when the points were added up, Blackmore Vale had won. Wembley here we come.

We set off for Wembley a week before the Show started, with the five ponies in Ron Mogg's lorry. The ponies were in temporary stabling at Wembley, and we were accommodated in caravans. The competition started on the Monday, and ran the whole week, culminating in the Grand Final on the Saturday evening. The five teams they were competing against were:-

Banwen and District
The Angus
The Peak
The Woodland
Eastern Harriers

The headline in the Horse & Hound, Nov 6th 1965 read;
Blackmore Vale Team Almost Brought the Roof Down.

Our Triumphant Team, from L to R:- Barry Mogg on Rusty, Linda Hoit on Nipper, Elsie Courage on Just Great, Susan Chaffey on Honeybee & Richard Dimond on Zeta, with their team trainer Mrs Hazel Harding.

On the Friday, the four teams with the most points went through to the Final the next day. After the Show had finished in the evening, we telephoned our friends and colleagues back home to tell them we had made the final. They all arrived on the Saturday morning in cars and buses to cheer our team on. When our youngsters entered the arena on the Saturday evening for the deciding heats, the roar from the crowd nearly brought the roof down.

When the last race was run there was a nail-biting wait while the Judges added up the points, and then the winners were announced. Blackmore Vale had won by 16 points. There wasn't a dry eye in our party, and all five of our team shed a tear as they proudly held up the Prince Philip Cup and made their lap of honour (*see photos*).

The following year, 1966, the Blackmore Vale Pony Club District Commissioner, Colonel Ian Balman and the Team trainer, Mrs. Hazel Harding decided it would be good to try to defend our title, but we had one problem. Both Elsie Courage and Barry Mogg had turned 16 and so were ineligible to compete, so two more members were required. Carol Mogg, Barry's sister, and Brenda Eavis were selected, and the practice started all over again. They did very well, and once again qualified for Wembley by winning the Zone Final at Butlins, Minehead. Come October up we all went again. They had good luck all week and got to the Grand Final on the Saturday. Both kids and ponies ran their hearts out. They were in the lead going into the last event when the girth on one of the saddles snapped sending the rider sprawling. She was unhurt, but it meant they lost that heat and ended up runners-up for the cup, losing by just two points. It was just very bad luck.

The 1966 Defending Pony Club Team from L to R:-
Linda Hoit on Nipper, Richard Dimond on Zeta, Susan Chaffey on Honeybee, Carol Mogg on Silver and Brenda Eavis on Blackie.

CHAPTER 5

Times Past

I shall never forget switching on electric light for the first time. It was in the early 1930's. All we ever had up 'til then was a paraffin lamp on our table, and all of us went to bed with a candle. You never saw electric lights in the streets, it was always gas lamps. The lamplighter came around with his ladder on a bicycle to light them each evening. Electric clocks were yet to come, like hundreds of other different gadgets. I think electricity has changed our lives in our homes more than anything in the last sixty years.

One summer we had a wedding in our family, and the bridegroom asked my mother if they could spend their first, (honeymoon) night at our house. She said, "Of course you can. That's no problem." While she was making up the bed she thought it would be a laugh to put a scrubbing brush in the bed. Also in those days, we always had a chamber pot under every bed as there were no toilets upstairs. After placing one each side of the bed, Mother thought it would be fun if she put $\frac{1}{2}$ a tin of Andrews Liver Salts in each pot. Being white china the crystals did not show up. When we had all had our supper, the newly weds went off to bed. We kept as quiet as we could, and all of a sudden the bride screamed. All those bubbles must have hit the right spot! We ended up having a good laugh.

A friend of mine was about to celebrate his 50th wedding anniversary so he asked his wife what she would like to do. She said, "I would like to go back to Cornwall and walk along that old railway line where we did our courting over 50 years ago." So off they went. They were walking along hand in hand like they had all those years ago, when his wife spotted an old fencing post. She said, "Can you remember, Fred, we made love for the very first time by that post?" He said, "So we did." On the way back they came to the post again, so they both thought it would be good fun to remember the past. After 10 minutes making love he asked his wife why she had come over so excited. She said, "Fred, fifty years ago that damn post was not electrified!"

On farms today you will find thousands of electric fences. They are used for keeping in cattle and sheep. They also keep dogs and foxes away from poultry. Farmers do not like too many dogs roaming in their fields. One of our sons had a dog come round that peed on their dustbin every morning when it went by for a walk. So he sat the dustbin on an old car tyre and put an electric fencer in the bin and set it going. The very next morning that dog had the biggest shock of his life. They said he must have run two miles down the road. The owner had to drag the dog past the bin the next morning.

You could always tell when people were getting up every morning. The first thing they did was light the fire to boil the kettle, and then fry the breakfast. Not many people have a good fried breakfast today.

There was a copper in almost every back kitchen to boil the washing. We had two coppers in our farmhouse kitchen. One was always lit. It was used for boiling gallons of hot water every day, which was needed on a farm. I remember every stitch of clothing we wore went in that copper, all the bed linen, eight or ten milking smocks, and babies' napkins, every week. It was taken out with a pair of tongs, then all put through a mangle (*see photo*) which we had to turn by hand, then hung out on the line in the garden every Monday to dry. You do not see all those lines of washing hanging out today. At Christmas you would see at least ten Christmas puddings, and two or three hams go in that copper. Everything that would burn went onto the fire. Old Wellington boots, hob-nail boots, bones and old brushes. I don't think we had a dustbin; there was no need for one. All the ashes went out onto the garden. All that smoke coming from the chimneys which you don't see today. About the only chimney you see smoke coming from these days is up at the crematorium.

I can remember when every village had a grave digger, and they always had a good story to tell. Only the other

A Washing Mangle

day I heard of a local family had an old aunt die out in Australia, so her ashes were sent back to this country for the burial in a Bisto tin. On the following Sunday afternoon the short service was arranged for the burial. After having their Sunday dinner they got ready to go up to the church. They looked everywhere for Aunt Fanny's ashes and could not find them. After telling everybody in the house they were on the mantle shelf in a Bisto tin one of the family cried out, "I used it to make the gravy for our dinner." Half the family burst out crying, and the other half laughed their heads off.

A well known farmer in this area, who died over 31 years ago was noted for his colourful language, most of which could not be repeated. We all went to his funeral. His wife survived him by another 30 years, and we also went to her funeral. About a week later I was talking to one of their sons. He told me that after his mother's funeral the family took the flowers up to the cemetery and laid them on their father's grave. One of his brothers whispered, "Father, we shall be bringing mother up to be with you soon." Another brother immediately replied, "You know what Father's going to say, don't you?" "No" everyone replied. "Hello mother, and where the !$#?*%=€¥¢s∫§¿ have you been for the last 30 years?

I knew an elderly farmer who only employed part-time work men. He had one who also happened to be the village grave digger. He never took any wages, so the farmer told him he could help himself to the cider that was kept in the barn. After a few months the farmer noticed this man was drinking more than his fair share, so he told him he did not need him any longer. The man became very upset, and he and the farmer had a good row. As he was leaving the farmyard he shouted out to this farmer, "When I dig your grave I'll see you go more than ten feet under." This played on the farmer's mind, and when he died I heard they had to bury him in the next village!

In the early 1940's there was an undertaker in Sherborne called Walter Penny, who lived in Hound Street. We knew him very well. We called him Uncle Walt. I went into his workshop one day and he was working on his bench under his own coffin. He told me it was the first thing he had ever made, so he was keeping it for himself. It was hanging from two short ropes up in the roof. In the summer he came up to our farm to help with the hay-making. One hot summer's night he was up on the hayrick with my father. We had lost a cast-iron seat off the hay rake, and the hay was going up that elevator so fast the seat was thrown into the elevator with the hay. As it came out on the hayrick it hit Uncle Walt on the head, knocking him out. We had to slide him down the ladder onto the ground. After a good twenty minutes he started to come around. All he kept shouting out was, "Tied up in the roof of my workshop." He did come around and lived a few more years. When Sherborne was bombed, (*see Chapter 3*) his house in Hound Street was badly damaged but his workshop at the rear of his garden was still standing and that coffin was still up there, waiting.

I remember Uncle Walt told me he had a young apprentice working for him and his first job was to lay out an old man that had died up at Pinford Farm. So off they both went on their bicycles. When they arrived at this cottage his wife said, "You'll find him upstairs in bed." So up they went. This young lad had never seen a dead person before. He told Uncle Walt he would be OK. When they arrived in the bedroom this old gentleman with a beard was sat up in bed, which made their job a bit more difficult to lay him out. So Walt told this young lad to press as hard as he could on both of the gentleman's knees, and he would pull his shoulders back. This was hard work. He had been dead for over twenty-four hours. They were doing well until Walt's hands slipped off his shoulders. This meant as he sprang forward he was bringing up wind, and his beard hit this young lad smack in the mouth. Uncle Walt said he had never seen anyone go down a flight of stairs so fast in all his life. He looked out of that bedroom window and saw a cloud of dust behind the lad's bicycle going back down Pinford Lane. He never saw that poor kid again.

About the only painter and decorator we had in Sherborne for some time was Stan Bow, who employed about twelve men full time. I remember one summer one of his men was decorating out our dining room. I think his name was Fred Mitchington. He had just finished papering the ceiling and was standing in the centre of the room admiring his handiwork, when all of a sudden the paper gave way. It fell from the ceiling and landed on his head. We could hear him shouting at the top of his voice "Stan, Stan, lend us a hand. If ever there was a poor unfortunate bugger, 'tis I."

A Cider Press

CHAPTER 6

Apple Days

In the early forties, the war was getting worse. Thousands of evacuees came to the West Country in hundreds of old charabancs, as we called them in the old days. We had a good apple orchard on our farm, and those kids had never seen so many apples in their lives. They were stripping the trees bare. One night, after tea, I went out in the orchard with my father. We saw two boys up one of the trees. Father found a good stick from the hedge, crept up the other side of the apple tree, and gave the boy a good crack across his ass. He fell out of the tree; Father caught him as he was running through the hedge, threw him on his shoulder and told him he would take him to the Police Station. After walking about two hundred yards Father could smell something. This poor kid was so frightened he'd messed himself.

He put him down on the ground and he ran away. When he arrived back in our kitchen I have never seen my mother laugh so much. Father's neck and his shirt collar were plastered. It taught him a lesson. He never went back out into that orchard for weeks, and the kids stripped every tree. We ended up buying cider the following year for haymaking and harvest.

We had two evacuees staying on the farm. They had the time of their lives. They came out in the barn one morning to see a calf being born. When it popped out one of the boys shouted out, "Look, George, it's already got hair!"

We made our own cider. We ground the apples and put them in the cider press (*see photo*). Almost every farmer had barrels of cider on their farms for their workers. I know our workers drank over one hundred gallons every summer at haymaking and harvest time.

When I was a young lad I remember some nights I had to go back home and fetch another jar full. One night one of the men let a young lad called Ted Warry taste a drop. He thought it was so good, when no one was looking he emptied the jar. He became so drunk he passed out. One of the men took him home in his old car. When we were having our supper, there was a knock on our back door. It was Ted's father. He demanded to see my father. Father went to the door, and was accused of getting Ted drunk. They ended up having a good row, and poor Ted was never allowed on our farm again.

One day, after a long days threshing at Bailey Ridge, Leigh, the two men that had been operating the thresher had consumed a large quantity of cider. They had just sheeted up for the night and set off on their bicycles for home. They hadn't got far when they realised they were very unsteady. Whilst pushing their bikes past a large manure heap they realised they could not go any further. So they left their bikes in a ditch, and crawled on to the top of the heap, where they both fell fast asleep.

The farmer spotted the two bikes when he went out to fetch the cows the next morning. They had spent the night up on the heap. With another day's work to do they had that thresher ready by 8 o'clock that morning.

These days, we very often get newcomers to the town complaining of the farm smells. So we tell them there are a lot of people up in the churchyard who would still love to smell it! It's events like this that country life is all about.

Everything we bought in Woolworth's cost 6d (2$\frac{1}{2}$p) or less. Petrol was 1s 4d (7p) a gallon. You could buy a new car for £100. Not many could afford one. I remember our very first car in 1937, an old Morris Cowley, TK 008, with a canvas roof. We gave £8 for it, drove it for the next six years, and it never cost us one penny, except fuel. In those days you never heard of a car having a service. They did not need one.

Almost every farmer had a stationary engine to operate a lot of their machinery. Among other jobs it was used for slicing up mangolds, cutting up chaff, cracking up cattle cake, (*see photo*), grinding up cider apples, kibbling and grinding corn, operating the elevator at hay-making time. They were mostly Lister and Petter engines run on petrol. Steam was on the way

Cake-cracking

out. You could operate a mill in those days with a water-wheel, not costing you a penny to run. If only we could make use of our rivers today. All we seem to use them for is pleasure. You never heard of anybody saying, "I'm fed up, or bored." Work was our hobby in those days, we enjoyed it. If we earned five shillings, (25p) a month, that was ours. The tax man was yet to come.

There are not many chimney sweeps left. Almost every chimney was swept once a year. In the 1940's we had neighbours called Mr. & Mrs. Warry. One day Mrs.Warry. was ill in bed, so her husband thought he would sweep the front room chimney. After ten minutes he thought he had screwed on a lot more rods than he

An old 'pit' privvy which can still be seen today on a local farm.

should have needed. Hearing his wife shouting out, "Help, come up quick," he ran up the stairs, only to find the head of the brush was out of the pot, plied over, and was coming through the bedroom window. This was the last chimney Rex Warry ever swept.

I remember we never had mains water in our house. We only had a hand pump out over a well in the garden, which never cost us a penny. The toilet was either a plank of wood with a large hole in it, over a bucket, (like ours was), or the plank was placed over a pit of lime (*see photo*) in a shed at the bottom of the garden. There was never any need to buy fertiliser in those days; we had ours on the premises. We had the best onions and rhubarb in town!

Today, too much fertiliser ruins the taste of a lot of everything we eat. Sprays were yet to come. I would far sooner eat a slug or two than be poisoned. Only those of us of the older generation know what good food really tastes like. We grew all the food we ate.

In Sherborne we had at least four large allotments, well over thirty acres in all. I remember delivering farmyard manure to most of them, especially when the war was on. Where have all the allotments gone? Almost every house in Sherborne had its own good vegetable garden. They had to, to live. All that digging kept us fit. We never had to complain. If we had back ache we just had to work it off, otherwise the family would starve. Today they try to keep fit by visiting the gym, or go jogging. People do not think about saving money to buy food. If they had to grow their own they would not know how to start. If there was ever another war I think most would die of starvation.

Supermarkets were yet to come. Now we have this so called organic food. A lot of our food today comes from other countries that do not have the same hygiene restrictions that the UK has. We have the strictest hygiene regulations in Europe. Unfortunately, some of our businesses have still to come up to standard.

I went into a fish and chip shop one evening recently, and I could see the server out the back pushing rubbish into a black plastic bin liner with her bare hands. She tied a knot in the top of the bag and left it beside two dustbins, at which point she spotted me waiting at the counter, and came in to serve me. I ordered my fish and chips, and watched her take my piece of fish from under the hot grill with her bare hands. When I got home, I had lost all interest in that fish, so I took it out in the garden and gave it to the cats. If I had reported her she would have lost her licence.

In the mid forties we used to ride our bicycles into town to see a film at the Carlton Cinema (*see photo*) in Higher Newland. We parked them in Bill Dewey's garage (*see photos*) for 1d and they were safe. The bicycle was the only way we could get around in those days. The 30mph signs were yet to come. Twenty five miles on a Sunday night was just down the road for us.

I remember my sister Nancy was riding her bike down Cheap Street one afternoon when she lost control, started swerving, and finally crashed into Fox's ice-cream three- wheeler (*see photo*). She ended up flat on her stomach on top of the cart. It shook her up so much Tom ended up giving her an ice-cream cornet to calm

The Carlton
Cinema

Dewey's Garage, Newland

Bill Dewey with his Wedding car.
(1931 Buick Straight 8 Limousine, 35 bhp)

her down. This same ice-cream man was always outside our school gate in Horsecastles every summer selling Fox's ice-creams, a penny a cornet. The same cornet today would cost you £1.

Fox's 3-Wheeler Ice Cream Cart, Tom Hann in Charge.
Fox's motto was 'Stop me and buy one better'.

CHAPTER 7

School Days

Almost everybody my age will tell you their school days were the best years of their lives. I never learned much at school, I never bothered. I must have got that cane more times than anybody in the school.

We were having a gardening lesson one afternoon when the Master asked me to name three of the seeds we planted in May. We all had to stand up to answer a question, so up I got and shouted out, "Let us turn up and pee!" (Lettuce, turnip and pea). The whole class were in fits of laughter, and I got the cane again.

One hot summer's afternoon a school mate of mine, Ron Chaffey, and I were picked by one of the masters to attend the bee hives in the school garden. Ron and I arrived at the hives before the master. We were not wearing our masks or hats. Ron asked me where the bees came out of. I said I did not know. Ron said, "Give the hive a kick." Like a damn fool I did. We had never seen so many bees come out of a hive in all our lives. We were surrounded by hundreds of them. Then they started to sting us. We both jumped straight through two rows of French beans which were already half way up the sticks. We ran as fast as we could to get out of the way, but the bees followed us in their hundreds. We were both getting stung in the head as we ran. We ended up in the shed at the bottom of the school garden. I remember we shut the door and sat on a heap of raffia. Both of us were crying our eyes out. Ron must have had more stings than me in the head. No-one found us for a good two hours. By this time both of us were in a bad way. Ron's head was so badly swollen he was taken to the Yeatman Hospital for treatment. I was not quite so bad.

One quiet afternoon in class, my best mate, who sat next to me, asked me to pull his finger. Like a damn fool I did. He came out with the loudest fart I have ever heard. The whole class was in fits of laughter. The master came charging over to us. He caught my mate by the scruff of the neck and called him a dirty gutter-snipe. He shook him so hard he let out two or three more. By then I was crying with laughter, so the master gave me a good clout too. It must have been a good ten minutes before he got the class back in order. We were both given five hundred lines each, but he did not know how to word them. He made sure we never sat together in class again. I remember having a half-crown ($22^{1}/_{2}$p) bet with my mate to see if he could do it again. Every time I looked across the classroom at him he would hold up one finger. What good laughs we had.

We used to walk up from Abbey School in Horsecastles, to Council School in Simons Road for woodwork, taught by a master. The girls were taught cookery by a lady teacher in the same building, which was a long wooden shed in the playground.

One afternoon the woodwork master lost his temper with me. I was not making full use of my hammer by holding it too close to the head. He shouted out to me. As I looked up I saw a wooden mallet coming directly at me, so I ducked. The mallet went straight through the window and out into the playground. He made me stay in after school to mend that window. I said, "It was not my fault, it was his. It was he that did it." He said it would not have happened if I had not ducked. A few weeks later I got my own back. I had a good wee in his petrol tank. He never got home very early that day.

Another day Ken Parks had lost his piece of wood he was working on, so the master sent him up to the timber shed to look for it. He did not come back. I was sent to look for him, and as I went through that door I heard a groaning sound. Ken was under a pile of planks that had fallen on him. He had removed the wrong piece of wood, thinking it was his. Four or five of us had to get him free. He was not too bad when we stood him up. A lot of my school pals have passed away, but I still have my memories.

Gwen and Beattie Hole at Elm Tree Farm, Holwell.
My mother's two younger sisters

CHAPTER 8

Reprieve

On a farm we were all taught at an early age to hand milk a cow (*see photo*), and almost all young lads had to learn an apprenticeship. We called it 'following an old dog'. You could learn far more by watching someone else than you ever will by pressing buttons, like youngsters do today. I started my apprenticeship when I was one year old. My mother sat me in an old cider barrel, half full of hay, on a rug, where I watched them hand milking cows. By the age of three I knew what it was I had to do. By the age of nine I was milking eight or ten cows a day. I had to, to pay for my keep. I went on to hand milk cows for the next forty years. Today you have to feed your kids, and then they expect pocket money as well, for doing nothing. Almost all young girls did an apprenticeship too. They went out to work in large houses as cooks and cleaners. It was called 'going out to service'. I bet there were a few good stories going around then. More than half the lads and lasses today do not even know what work they want to do when they reach the age of twenty. In our early days you always found the poorest families were always the happiest. The doctors in those days always said the kids that were brought up in the country were always the healthiest, because they lived a bit rougher, and were immune to almost all diseases. I am absolutely sure the food we ate in those days had a lot to do with it, as we knew where it came from. A lot of our food today comes from other countries, and the sad part is we do not know what half of it is. If we had another war, and all our imports were stopped, I think most of our inhabitants would die of starvation. In my school days, the boys were taught gardening, and the girls had cookery lessons. What a good start in life. Have you noticed how much more expensive our food is becoming? It would not be a bad idea if our younger generation learnt to grow and prepare their own food. They might have to one day.

REPRIEVE

As turns the plough a furrow straight
To bring the people bread,
The farmers toil upon their soil
And God is overhead.
No rest for man or beast
Until the work be done,
The harvest safely gathered in
And hidden from the Hun.

These men who twice in three decades
Have saved the Nation's life,
Remembered not, were left to rot,
Forgotten in their strife.
Small wonder be that few were found
But very ill-prepared,
Yet heard the call and taking stand
Their tasks and labour shared.

Throughout the land the tractors' roar
Upon the wind is borne,
Like days of old, the fields are gold
And thick with ripening corn.
The herdsmen work within the byre,
Each shepherd on his hill,
A varied throng of yeomen folk
But with one single will.

And how the land that once was sick
Shall feed the sons she bore,
Once more the toil upon the soil
Has helped to fight a war.
God made the land that man should live,
The Devil bids him kill,
Twice warned the Nation stands reprieved
Neglect shall bode us ill.

In the 1930's we had a young farm lad working for us. We kept a few ducks in those days, and my mother wanted to rear a few more. As we did not have a drake to run with these ducks, she asked this lad if he would walk out to Farmer Gold's farm in Oborne, and bring her back a drake that Mr.Gold said she could borrow. Off he went. He must have mistaken what my mother had told him. The silly bugger arrived back with a hay rake.

After we found the damned 'hay rake' was no good, I went off to Sturminster Newton market and bought a hen with 14 young ducklings, in the hope I might end up one day with some laying ducks. The reason we use hens to hatch duck eggs is because the hen can cover more eggs when sitting than a duck. Young ducks grow very fast, and when they were about twelve weeks old I noticed they all looked the same. You can usually tell the ducks from the drakes by their feathers. A few weeks later I met the young farming friend of mine who I'd purchased them from. I told him I was not very happy with the ducklings I'd bought as it looked like they were all young drakes. He said, "Yes, they are. We sexed them all at one day old!" That's what we used to call 'having the gift of the gab', but we're still good friends to this day.

In the early days on a farm, we used to sell hundreds of Hessian bags that our cattle food came in. The bag man came round about once a month. This was my pocket money. He arrived one fine morning in April, and spotted a lot of wild pigeons in our first field, feeding on the young clover. He told me he would drop in the next week and show me the way to catch them. Being a young lad I was longing to see what he meant. His name was Mr. Fred Wright, and he lived in Yeovil.

He arrived a week later in his old red Cheviot lorry. As he got out of the lorry I noticed he was carrying two pigeon decoys, and some black twine. On this he had about forty green peas tied on it at one foot apart. He asked me if the pigeons still came out there, and I said, "Yes, they do." So out he goes in the field and set up the two decoys and made one large circle with this twine with all those peas tied to it. He then said we must get out of sight, so we did. After a good ten minutes those pigeons were flying in. Then more kept coming. There must have been over twenty, all pecking up those peas. He told me to walk out and clap my hands, so I did. As they flew up with all those peas in their crops the twine became entangled in their wings. They managed to get about 500 yards, then they all came down in a large thorn hedge. All we could see was a cloud of feathers. When I got out there they were all half plucked. I remember ending up with sixteen pigeons, already plucked. All that fun on our farms is sadly disappearing.

I knew a young man who got engaged to a young lady, and he could not decide what to buy her for Christmas. So he went out shopping with his sister. On entering the draper's shop she bought a pair of knickers for herself and he bought a pair of gloves for his lady love. A 'little error' occurred in sending the parcel off, with the result that the knickers were sent to his young lady instead of the gloves, along with the following letter –

My dearest Mabel

    I do hope you will accept this little token instead of a silly Christmas card.

    How I wish no other hand would touch them after you put them on. I know, dearest, that such a wish is in vain as thousands of young men may touch them and other eyes than mine may see them on you. I bought the smallest size I could get and if they are too large then let them wrinkle down a bit. Always wear them when we are out together, as I want to see if they fit you.

    My sister says she has to clean hers once a month as so many young men soil them with their hands, but you can clean them with benzoin if you leave them on to dry. I do hope, dear, that they are not too small, and be careful, dear, not to wet them, and be sure to blow in them before you put them on.

With all my love

Sidney.'

CHAPTER 9

My Young Farmers Club days

I was a member of the Sherborne Young Farmers Club. What fun we had. All those farm visits, talks, and entertainments. My sister Nancy and I attended the very first meeting in 1939, at the Eastbury Hotel, Sherborne, and twenty years later Sherborne Club became the largest club in Dorset, with over one hundred members at one time (*see photo*). I feel honoured to be a life member of that club, and I am still involved with the Young Farmers today (*see photo*). At one time there were over forty clubs in Dorset alone. Our three sons have all been Chairmen of our club, and Robert became County Chairman in 1978/79. We were having tea one afternoon when he told us his job that night was to pick a new County organiser, as four young girls had applied for the job. We asked him the following morning who he had picked. I remember him saying, "Dad, she's a smasher! Her name is Christina Cluett." What a good choice that was, as he ended up marrying her eighteen months later.

Sherborne Young Farmers Harvest Supper, Yetminster - 1948

Sherborne Young Farmers at the Rally, Beaminster – 1947
L to R:- Maud Chaffey, Doug Atfield, Sylvia Coffin, Jack Dimond, Joyce
Gawler, Nancy Dimond, Kitt Joliff, Marjery Griffiths.

They held a rally once a year, where every club in Dorset took part. They were held on the larger farms all over the county. All the boys and girls took part in every competition you could think of (*see photo*). There is a Rally Shield presented every year to the Club with the highest points for their competition entries, (*see photo*). Sherborne Young Farmers Club won the shield no less than ten times between 1955 and 1990. What fun they all had.

After the war, with petrol rationed, the County Rally was held at Puddletown, so Sherborne YFC decided to hire a bus for the day as we were having a dance that evening back in the Corn Exchange, Dorchester. So we hired a bus from Macklins of Sherborne.

Richard Dimond, Dave Norman, Peter Potter & Richard Jesty with their version of 'Swan Lake'

Sherborne YFC winning the Rally Shield – 1971
L to R – Sylvia Coffin, Joyce Dibble, Pat Harris, Roger Hole, Ann
Kingman, Marigold Jesty, Robert Brown(President), Marilyn Bunter,
Roy Kingman, Ivan Croad, Angela Hole, Hilary Tinsley(County
Organiser), Robert Dimond, the Author & Ian Dimond

There were about forty of us left Sherborne early that morning.

At the Rally there was a skittle alley, and the prize for the top score was a live pig. It was a good pig, about twelve weeks old. I kept pigs at the time, and was hoping to win it. Later that afternoon I was told I had, and I thought 'how the hell am I going to get it home', so I sold it to Tony Young for £2.00. He found a large Hessian bag to put it in, and made his way back to the coach. The driver was not very happy.

When we arrived back in Dorchester for the dance, the pig had to be left on the coach. Around 11.30 pm that evening two policemen came into the Corn Exchange and stopped the dancing, got up on the stage, and asked if anyone in the room owned a pig? Tony coloured up, but eventually confessed to owning the pig. The police told him it had just run off down the main street and cars were swerving all ways. About six of us went out and finally caught it on the river bridge at the lower end of town. When we arrived back at the coach, we found the pig had eaten its way out of the sack and had been running up and down between the seats. The coach smelled like a pig sty as the pig had messed and peed all over the place. When our coach driver woke up from his nap, he was very angry. Being a town man he had never smelled anything like it in his life. We noticed he was looking very pale, then, suddenly, he lost everything he had eaten that day. I offered to drive the coach home, but he wouldn't let me. We set off for Sherborne with every window in the coach open. A few weeks later my mother met the driver in town. He told her, "It was the worst day

I have ever experienced. A month later that coach still stank, and I refused to take it out again." We thought afterwards, the only person who could have let that pig off the coach was the driver! That is just one of the dozens of stories I could tell you.

I remember Robert entered a bottle of Rhubarb wine one year. On the way to the rally the bottle got smashed, and he and the other two boys he had in the car with him decided to stop at the next village shop to buy a bottle of Tizer, as they were thirsty. After drinking the Tizer, they thought it would be a good idea if they stuck the Rhubarb wine label on the bottle, and fill the bottle with pee! So they all took it in turns, then stuck the cork from the smashed bottle in the top. When the judging was over, they were allowed back in the building to see the results. Robert made straight for the wine table, only to find he had been awarded 'Highly Commended'. Those three boys laughed all the way home.

For the Young Farmers Ploughing Competition, Robert won the 'under 21' Class for Dorset on two occasions. He also won the 'under 25' Class for Dorset three times (*see photo*). Robert was also the representative for Dorset in three National Finals, which were held in Surrey, Hereford and Kent.

Ian has always had a good eye for judging stock and was successful at showing cattle and pigs. He was chosen to represent Dorset in the National Stockman of the Year competition several times (*see photo*). On two occasions he reached the National Final held at Smithfield Show, coming fourth and fifth respectively from an estimated 10,000 initial competitors. In one year Robert and Ian

Robert with some of his cups

Ian with his Stockman's Trophies, 1979

Some of the 30 plus cups Robert & Ian won in one year

won over thirty cups between them *(see photo)*.

Sadly, today, Young Farmers Clubs all over the country have declined, as most of the farms have been forced to sell up. In the last twenty five years 75% of our young farmers have disappeared. In 1950 about 97% of farmers' sons took up farming. Today it is less than 5%. I think it is very sad, and I do think the day will come when our country will need us. However there are still a lot of very good Young Farmers Clubs in our country today, and I would strongly advise any young lad or lass between the ages of fourteen and twenty-five to join. They need not be farmers' sons or daughters. If they have a club nearby, just ring up, then go along. It will be the best thing they ever do. They do not know what fun they are missing.

I think one of the biggest achievements Sherborne Young Farmers had was winning the National finals of the Entertainment Competition one year. This was a half an hour variety show *(see photo)*, where they had to win all the preliminary rounds to get through to the final, which was held at Blackpool. The first heat was held in Sturminster Newton, where they were up against four other clubs, Sherborne was judged the winners. The second heat was at Weymouth Pavilion where they took on four more clubs and won again. The third heat was at Newquay Pavilion, where they took on the winning clubs from the whole of Cornwall.

The semi-final heat was up at Tewkesbury, where they met four other clubs who had also won their county preliminary rounds. This they also won, which put them through to the final at the Blackpool Opera House, where

The Cast of "Holiday Hotel" - 1977
Back row: Derek Hole, Sarah Wilson, Paul Carter, Alan Tizzard, Sally
Pearce, Nicola Clarke, Ian Dimond, Vanessa Goodland, Graham Fudge,
Sue Key, Terence Myles, Stephen Harris.
Front row: Gill Thornton, Sue Fudge, Robert Dimond, Pauline Tizzard &
Glenys Congrave.

they were competing against the other four best clubs in the country. They were drawn first to go on stage. The boys and girls from Sherborne Young Farmers club almost brought the roof down. After the four other clubs had performed, and the judges had made their final decision, Sherborne YFC were awarded the winners (*see photo*). We were all very proud of our sons and daughters, when they arrived home on the bus the next day with the cup. At our house we had the flags flying, and streamers across the road, and we celebrated with champagne.

"We Won!"
L to R: Gill Thornton, Robert Dimond, Paul Goodfellow, Peter West, Sue Fudge, Ian Dimond, Alan Tizzard, Myra Newman, Sally Pearce, Paul Carter, Nicky Clarke, Derek Hole, Stephen Harris, Terence Myles, Pauline Tizzard, Vanessa Goodland, Graham Fudge, Sue Key, Glenys Congrave & Sarah Wilson.

SHERBORNE Y.F.C. (DORSET)

'HOLIDAY HOTEL'

Producer: Peter West

CAST

Hotel Manager: Paul Goodfellow
On the Beach: Entire Cast
Deckchair Attendant: Robert Dimond
Greek Dance: Paul Goodfellow, Gill Thornton, Sue Fudge, Pauline Tizzard, & Glyn Congrave,
Waiters: Terence Myles, & Alan Tizzard,
Three Char Ladies: Graham House, Ian Dimond, & Graham Fudge,
Ted & Maggie: Robert Dimond & Nicola Clarke
Solo: Sue Fudge
Chef: Robert Dimond
                           Sue, Pauline & Paul
Harold: Robert Dimond
Finale: Paul Goodfellow, Robert Dimond, Gill Thornton, Sue Fudge, Pauline Tizzard, Glyn Congrave, Terence Myles, Alan Tizzard, Graham House, Ian Dimond, Graham Fudge, Nicola Clarke, Vanessa Goodland, Alan Foot, Michael Gurston,
Stephen Harris, Gregory Kellaway,   Sally Pearse & Sarah Wilson.
Make-up: Beverley Hole
Pianist: Sue Key

Sherborne Y.F.C. show the daily routine of a typical holiday hotel and reveal their guests on holiday

The Programme at Blackpool

CHAPTER 10

Nature's Wonders

We used to have to buy a licence to keep a dog, now the silly buggers pay some people to keep one, and some can't even keep themselves. Can it get much dafter?

I think health and fitness centres are a waste of time, as most people today are happy doing nothing. Aids was equipment to help older people with a disability. Now it is a disease you catch. We always thought the MasterCard was a playing card. Nowadays it is a piece of plastic.

Today most of our youngsters do not know what an oak tree, or an ash tree, or a thistle is. You often hear them say they are bored. In our time board was a plank of wood.

I was born too soon. When we were married we were

given wedding presents; probably a chamber pot to go under the bed. Today they would expect to be given the whole bedroom suite!

The auctioneers in Sherborne were Messrs. Senior and Godwin. We had a weekly cattle market which was held every Thursday. It was on the site where Market car park is now. During my working life I have taken hundreds of calves and pigs up there to sell. Some of the cattle I sold

The Weighbridge

had to go down to the weighbridge to be weighed first. The weighbridge, which is 18th Century, was in Half Moon Street, in front of the Abbey (*see photo*). The actual weighing plate was removed in 1950, but the little half-round building which houses the weighing mechanism can still be seen.

Once a month Senior and Godwin held an auction in the Swan Inn sale rooms. My sister was interested in dress-making, so one day, at the sale, she purchased a dress-maker's dummy. One winter's night she left it at the top of the stairs. I arrived home very late that night, creeping up the stairs in the dark, so as not to wake anybody, just feeling my way with my hands. I ended up with my arms around this damned dummy. I had never shaken so much in all my life. I thought it was someone standing up there, so I gave it one good wallop, knocking it down the stairs, waking up everyone in the house in the process. When they put the lights on, we found the damned thing was smashed in about six pieces. My sister bawled her eyes out.

In the 40's and 50's the local copper was the farmer's best friend. I remember one winter's night, a young farming friend of mine and I went off to a dance at Glanvilles Wootton. He came over in the dinner hour to tell me he would drive his father's car, which was a black Austin 16. I said, "No, you will surely get caught, as you are only fifteen years old!" He arrived over about 8 o'clock, sitting on three cushions, so he could see over the steering wheel! I came out of the hall that night about 11-30 pm to see a copper stood by his car. I went back in to tell my friend. He said, "Don't worry, we will be OK." We both got in the car to come home, when this copper came over to ask him for his Driving Licence. He opened his wallet and gave him a Driving Licence. It was his father's! When he spotted the surname, the copper said, "OK." So we drove home. That was when you knew who your friends were.

Years ago ladies kept their handkerchiefs up their knicker legs, and when they sneezed it was called a 'tishoo'. Retrieving their hankies became a bit embarrassing, so then paper tissues came on the market in cardboard boxes to save the ladies modesty.

Saturday nights were always 'bath nights'. Us kids took it in turns in a long tin bath up in the back kitchen. Our mother scooped the warm water out of the old copper with a tin bucket. We could splash about as much as we liked because the kitchen floor was all old blue stone flags, no heaters or floor coverings in those days.

Holidays nowadays are taken abroad. I remember going on my first holiday on a farm with two of my cousins. They were both girls, and we were about five years old. When Saturday night came round, my Auntie brought the old tin bath into the back house. To my surprise she dumped all three of us in together, and told us to give each other a good scrubbing! She said she would come back later. I was hoping she would not be back for some time, as I kept on 'losing' the soap, and was having the time of my life fishing for it. Then in comes my aunt. She told the girls to hop out and she would dry them off with the towel. That was the first time I had ever seen two young girls with no clothes on. I could not believe what I was looking at! When they were both dried off, their mother said, "Tis your turn now, Jack." I said, "Please could I dry myself," as I was far too embarrassed and afraid to stand up. I went completely berserk. When everything had settled down again I got out. You never forget the first one you see, and I saw two!!

When I was eight years old, I went on a holiday up on one of my aunt and uncle's farms in Stourpaine. The first morning after having breakfast I asked my Auntie where the toilet was. She said, "That little house at the end of the garden path." Just before I left she said, "Try not to wake up the broody hen. She's in there sitting on thirteen hens eggs." I found this very hard to do, as my aunt had given me a dish of prunes for my breakfast! I can still see this hen today, sat there in an old clothes basket. Two mornings later my aunt said, "I will come out with you as they are due to hatch out today." I shall never forget as my Auntie lifted the hen out of the basket it was full of chicks. When we counted them there were sixteen. Three of those eggs must have been double yolkers.

When our three sons were young they kept every animal you could think of. About the only one they never brought home was a monkey. They arrived home one day with a tortoise which they kept losing, so I drilled a hole in its shell, and they tied it on with a long piece of string. They came in upset one day. 'Tortie' was missing. The piece of string had snapped right by its shell. It had been tethered on a piece of waste ground beside the railway line. Four years later a man was walking down the railway line with a bucket in his hand. It was one of the railway workers. He asked me if I knew anyone who had lost a tortoise. I said, "No." Then after a few minutes I remembered the tortoise our boys had lost, so I shouted out, "It might be ours." After having a good look at the shell, the hole I had drilled four years ago was still there, so I asked, "Where did you find it?" He said, "Just this side of Templecombe Station." That tortoise travelled over four miles in four years!

Animals have a marvellous sense of direction. We bought a cow in Yeovil Cattle Market one Friday. On the Saturday morning she was missing. A farmer from Marston Magna, which was over five miles away, rang us to tell us she had arrived back in his yard. That cow had never been off his farm before, and had travelled overnight to get there.

We were having a day's shooting at Charlton Horethorne one winter's day, when one of our beaters lost his dog. He whistled and shouted in every field, but he could not find his dog. When he arrived home at Shepton Montague he found his dog lying on the lawn. That dog had travelled over six miles. I have been told a lot of animals have been known to travel much further than that.

I remember a Mr. Bill Prout that lived in Westbury, in Sherborne. He had his own cattle lorry. He did all our livestock hauling to markets. One day he gave me his old army rifle, which he had brought back from the Boer War. He told me the last thing he had shot with it was a sniper who had raided their camp one dark night, and cut off the ears of four of our men! The next morning he told me he and two others were sent out to look for this sniper. He said, "I was sat under a large oak tree, when I noticed a few leaves were dropping around me. As I slowly looked up I saw the sniper sat up there. We were always told never to pull the trigger if you can't see his head. All I could see was his ass! I was getting so nervous, so I took aim. When I pulled the trigger he fell out of the tree, landing right by my feet. He was dead. I noticed blood was coming from his head, and that bullet went up his ass and out of the top of his head. I was presented with a medal for shooting him in the head!" I used that rifle for years shooting rabbits and birds.

For several years I raced greyhounds, my best one being a dog called 'Jimmer'. When 'Jimmer' had reached the end of his racing career I used him for catching rabbits. On a wet and windy night that dog would pick up forty to fifty rabbits. I would be carrying a powerful torch with a spot bulb, so I had a good beam of about one hundred yards. I then could keep the light on the rabbit until the dog had caught it. He would immediately bring it back to me, and then I would look for the next one. It was great fun.

One of my cousins, John Strange, had one of the best greyhounds I have ever seen (*see photo*). On a good, rough, windy night he would catch fifty or sixty rabbits. John came in one night with his dog, 'Fly', and we both went out with the light. We had not gone far before the dog had caught twenty rabbits. All of a sudden he started barking, something he had never done before. Then he immediately ran off in the direction of Crackmore Wood, a mile away. We thought he must have had a fit, so we took off after him, but we never found him. John went home to Pulham that night very upset. He came back the next day and walked every field, but no luck, so he decided to stay at our house. A good week went by, and then one morning in thick fog, he came across the dog lying under a hay rick in the very same field we'd lost him in over seven days ago. He was not in very good condition, but after a bit of nursing, he was back on form again in two weeks.

My cousin's dog, 'Fly'

We always had one or two other dogs on our farm. They never cost us much to keep, as we always had dead calves. One calf would last three dogs a good ten days, and we always had milk from the cows, which was not good enough to go in the milk churns. Those dogs were always fit. They had to be, to keep foxes away from the farmyard at night. One fox will kill twenty to thirty hens in one visit. Not a pleasant sight. They also carry away thousands of newly born lambs and pigs every year. I went out one dark night to see a cow in a field that was due to have her calf. I shone my torch on her and I could not believe my eyes. There were two foxes on the rear end of that cow fighting over that calf that was only halfway born. I was just in time to save it. You can see why farming is a twenty-four hour a day job.

One summer a large section of our pig sty wall fell out in the farmyard, so two of the Digby Estate men were sent out to repair it. They were Harry Axe, and Harry Cane, who was the Estate stonemason. When they arrived they saw our Devon bull in his pen, which was adjoining this wall. They were very scared, as this bull was roaring at them. With no other safe pen to shut him in, he had to stay put. On the second morning they had just mixed up a large quantity of cement in a wheelbarrow, when they saw this bull walking towards them. He had knocked back the bolt on his door and let himself out. They ran inside the pig sty and shut the two doors. The bull started roaring again, and pawing the ground, where he managed to spread five tons of sand over the yard. Then he started on the cement. Six bags of Portland cement went straight over his head. The wheelbarrow with the cement mixture was next. The bull smashed it to pieces. The two men were peeping out through one of the doors, shaking like leaves. They were too afraid to speak, as they might be next. After about two hours one of our men walked into the yard. He saw the bull, let a cow out into the yard to calm him down, then drove them both to a safe place. It took the two Harrys the rest of the day to clean up the mess, and Len Hart, the carpenter in the Estate yard, had to make them a new wheelbarrow, which were all wood in those days. The metal wheelbarrows with rubber wheels were yet to come. Two other workmen were sent out to finish the wall. Harrys Axe and Cane told us it was the longest two hours of their lives.

CHAPTER 11

A Farming Dynasty

Most families were large in the early 1900's. My father, Frank Dimond, was one of six children, four boys and two girls, who, when married, all worked on their own farms. My mother, whose maiden name was Hole, was one of fifteen children, all brought up on a small farm in the village of Holwell (*see photo*). My mother's father was William Hole (*see photo*), who was born in Henstridge in 1866, and who married Lucy Hann of Yetminster on 18th May, 1892. Their first farm was Hartmore Farm, Pulham. In 1897 they moved to Hill Street Farm, Holwell, where they spent the next forty years. I am proud to say 106 years later it is still farmed by the same family. Richard Hole, (*see photo*) with his

The Hole Family

William Hole with his Gloucester spot pigs

Richard Hole outside the farmhouse as it is today

son Robert still have the tenancy, which makes it the fourth generation working the same farm. At one time there were eight farms on the Digby Estate all farmed by descendants of the late William Hole. All fourteen children attended the same village school. Every morning they walked across three or four fields to get there in their lace-up hob-nailed boots. At one time there were seven of them attending at the same time. I dread to think how the mothers today would cope if they had to get that lot ready for school, and prepare all those midday lunches. I was told some of the boys took bread and cheese and a pint of cider, while the girls took sandwiches and a bottle of milk. It was that or nothing in those days. I am pleased that Holwell School is still being used to this day as a Play School *(see photo)*.

Holwell Village School

These were their fifteen children

Francis Sarah	Dec. 4th	1892	4 children
William George	Jan 14th	1894	Killed in action in France Mar 21st, 1918
Hilda	Jul 19th	1895	no children
Henry James	Oct 5th	1896	3 children
Clara Beatrice	Jan 19th	1899	2 children
Florence Elsie	Aug 19th	1900	3 children
Phyllis Lily	Dec 4th	1901	3 children
Eva	Mar 30th	1903	Died from measles age 2 years
Anne Laura	Dec 24th	1904	2 children
Allan Robert	Mar 1st	1906	1 child
Reginald Sydney	Nov 28th	1907	3 children
Gwendoline Alice	Apr 23rd	1909	2 children
Olive	Oct 27th	1911	no children
Albert John} twins	April 30th	1913	2 children
Benjamin Edward}			3 children

Most of the boys married and went on to be farmers, and almost all the girls were married in Holwell Church. Every one of them could hand-milk a cow, and some were sent to other farms as cheese-makers. Sure enough, when they married they all worked on a farm for the rest of their lives.

William Hole, like most farmers in those days, had his own special cider mug. We still have that cider mug today (*see photo*). It must be well over one hundred years old, and held a quart (two pints) of cider. The old farmers could manage four or five of these mugs full in

The inscriptions on the mug are as follows:

Let the Wealthy and Great
Roll in Splendor and State,
I envy them not I declare it:
I eat my own lamb,
My Chickens and Ham,
I shear my own Fleece & I wear it.
I have lawns I have Bow'rs
I have Fruits, I have Flow'rs,
The Lark is my morning alarmer:
So jolly Boys now
Here's God speed the Plough.
Long Life & Success to the Farmer

He that by the Plough Would Thrive
Himself must Either Hold or Drive
God Speed the Plough

In God is Our Trust

The Farmers' Arms

one night. The cider cost very little, as most farmers made their own.

William Hole's Cider Mug on a Staddlestone

Also still seen around the county are staddle stones (*see photo*). Although mainly used in gardens for ornamental purposes now, they were originally used to support hay ricks. Long poles were placed across from stone to stone, and the rick built on the poles, thus keeping the hay/straw off the ground, and preventing the rats from getting in and building nests.

Corn Ricks up on Staddlestones in the late 19th Century

William Hole died on April 30th, 1935, aged 69 years and Granny Hole (Lucy) died on September 21st 1960, aged 86 years. Their eldest son, William George, was called up in the First World War, and he set off on his own horse with the Dorset Yeomanry. He later transferred to the 6th Battalion Somerset Light Infantry, attaining the rank of Lance Corporal. On his last night in England he stabled his horse at Castle Farm, and slept in our farmhouse, which at that time was the home of the Johnson family. The next morning he and Elias Johnson set sail for France. The two photographs were taken outside our stable door. William George was killed in action in France on March 21st, 1918, his name can be seen at Pozieres Memorial, Somme, France, Ref. Panels 25 & 26. Pozieres is a village 6 kilometres north-east of Albert.

William George Hole outside the stable door

Elias Johnson outside the stable door

The following was taken from a local paper that year:-

Hole. In ever loving memory of our dear son and brother, William George, killed in action on March 21st, 1918, aged 23 years.

> He sleeps beside his comrades
> In a grave across the foam.
> He lives in the hearts that loved him
> And those he has left at home.

As he lived, so he died. One of the bravest. Still sadly missed by all. Hill Street Farm, Holwell.

This poem was written on a scrap of paper, picked up in France and sent home to my mother. The author was never known.

A Soldier's Prayer Before Battle

> Stay with me God, the night is dark,
> The night is cold: My little spark
> Of courage dies. The night is long,
> Be with me God, and make me strong.
> I love a game, I love a fight,
> I hate the dark, I love the light,
> I love my child, I love my wife,
> I am no coward, I love life.
> I know that death is but a door,
> I know what we are fighting for.

Peace for the kids, our brothers freed,
A kinder world, a cleaner breed.
I'm but the son my mother bore,
A simple man and nothing more.
But – God of strength and gentleness

Be pleased to make me nothing less.
Help me O God when death is near
To mock the haggard face of fear.
That when I fall – if fall I must
My soul may triumph in the dust.

There was a family reunion on 27th June, 1981 at Alweston Village Hall. It was a gathering of one of the largest farming families in the area. There were 150 Holes, all descendants of the late Mr. & Mrs. William Hole. At the party were ten of the surviving children (*see photo*), plus 36 grandchildren and about 100 great grandchildren and great, great grandchildren. Ages ranged from six weeks to 88 years. If they had all attended there would have been over 200 members, and I discovered I had twenty-five first cousins.

Ten of the following couples ended up farming their own farms.

The Hole Family Marriages

Francis Sarah Catherine	Tom Ford
Henry James (Jim)	Ethel May Yeatman
Clara Beatrice (Beattie)	Victor Patch
Florence Elsie Susanna (Flo)	Reginald Stranger
Phyllis Lily Mary (my mother)	Frank Dimond (my father)
Anne Laura	Albert Stokes (Bert)
Allan Robert	Veta Harris
Reginald Sydney (Reg)	Ada Harris
Gwendoline Alice (Gwennie)	Frederick Heath
Olive	William Lane
Albert John (Jack)	Emily Burt (Millie)
Benjamin Edward (Ben)	Adelaide Eastment (Girlie)

The last of the fifteen to pass away from that large family was Gwen on March 5th 2002, at the age of 92 years.

The ten surviving Hole children at reunion party.
From left standing:- Alan Hole, Mrs Beatrice Patch, Ben Hole, Mrs Olive Lane, Mr Reg Hole.
Sitting from left:- Mrs Francis Ford, Mrs Gwen Heath, Mrs Phyllis Dimond, Mrs Annie Stokes, Miss Hilda Hole.

Working in a farmyard years ago used to be the happiest place on earth. Now, with all the red tape and bureaucracy it has become one of the saddest places to be today. If we lose our country sports, like shooting, hunting and fishing, it would be the end of country life.

Not many years ago, the day of a farm sale was the saddest in a farmer's life, especially if it had been in the family for several generations. Nowadays it is often the happiest, as the farmer can no longer make his living at it. Why should he have to work a 70 plus hour week just to feed his family?

Discipline has also gone. In our younger days there were far more honest people around we could trust and respect. Almost all deals were done on the shake of a hand. It is a far different story today, where lawyers and solicitors are involved and industrial espionage is commonplace. I am sure discipline starts in the home, around the kitchen table. Remember learning your P's and Q's? 'Yes please' and 'No thank you' were the first rules we learnt before we ever started school. By then it's too late. If it doesn't improve, along with respect for other people and their property, I dread to think what this country will be like in five years time. With ever more burglaries, muggings and violent crimes, our prisons will never cope.

Before many more years I think farming will come full circle. The reason being almost everything we purchase is getting more and more expensive. I think the day will come when people have to cut down on their cost of living. It is already starting to go that way.

Every day we hear of city-dwellers buying up a farm

house with land and deserting the city so they can keep a cow, a pig, hens and ducks, and a horse or two. We could end up where we were seventy years ago, back in the good old days. Here's hoping!

The hardest thing I now have to do is to sit and watch someone else doing the work I used to do.

I'm nearly 80!

Today dear Lord, I'm 80, there's much I haven't done
So I hope dear Lord you'll let me live until I'm 81.

But then if I haven't finished what I want to do
Would you let me stay a while until I'm 82?

So many places I want to go, so very much to see –
Do you think you could manage to make it 83?

The world is changing fast, there is so much in store
I'd like it very much to live until 84

And if by then I'm still alive
I'd like to stay till 85

More plans will be up in the air so I'd really like to stick
And see what happens when I'm 86.

Dear Lord it's much to ask (it might be nice in Heaven)
But I really would like to stay until I'm 87

I know by then I won't be fast and sometimes I'll be late
But it would be very pleasant to be here at 88

I will have seen many things and had a wonderful time
So I'm sure that I will be willing to leave at 89

May be!

Copies of this book are available from:

Mr W. J. Dimond
Toll Cottage,
Oborne Road,
Sherborne,
Dorset DT9 3RY
Tel. 01935 813701

and all good bookshops.

—

Printed by Remous Ltd, Milborne Port, Sherborne Dorset DT9 5EP